PORTSMOUTH HISTORIC DOCKYARD

WELCOME to Portsmouth Historic Dockyard, home of the Royal Navy and part of Britain's premier naval base.

Entering Victory Gate you follow in the footsteps of kings, queens and admirals besides the numerous seamen, soldiers and dockyardmen who kept Britain's navy at sea, protecting the shipping lanes of the world and defending the realm. Imagine Captain Cook returning from his circumnavigation of the world in 1775 and Admiral Nelson preparing for the Battle of Trafalgar in 1805.

Beyond the gateway you enter the mainly Georgian Dockyard, for centuries inaccessible to visitors. Now the setting for three historic ships *Mary Rose*, HMS *Victory*, HMS *Warrior* and the Royal Naval Museum, this Dockyard was once the largest industrial complex in the world.

WE HOPE YOU ENJOY YOUR VISIT

Portsmouth Historic Dockyard

King John's order is the first clear description of the infant dockyard that was to grow, over the centuries, to become Britain's premier naval base.

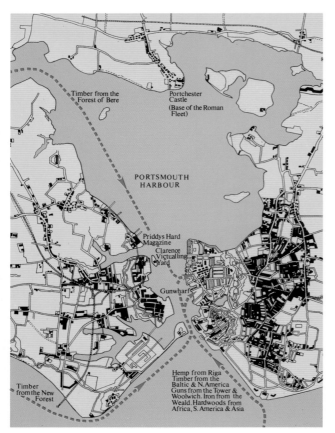

Portsmouth Dockyard was connected by water to other shore establishments and received supplies from many countries

WHAT IS A DOCKYARD?

A Royal Dockyard is owned by the Crown and has all the skills, crafts and facilities to tackle any task involved in ship building or repair, including the day to day running of warships. In contrast a civilian shipbuilding yard may construct a ship's hull and perhaps the engines. Once the ship was completed she would probably never return to that yard.

Within Portsmouth Dockyard with its wharfs, dry docks and storehouses, the crafts have their own workshops and material stores capable of tackling any job required for building or repairing ships and their equipment.

During your visit you will see the splendid survival of Georgian storehouses, ropehouse, boathouses and office blocks together with dry docks and the Great Ship Basin. The setting is evocative of many centuries of naval history.

A COMPLEX ESTABLISHMENT

When metal ship construction and steam power succeeded sail, large workshops were needed to house foundries, armour plate shops and later factories where turbines and equipment for the great gun turrets were made.

There were also extensive ranges of storehouses from which Dockyard and ships' officers could draw anything from lifeboats to scrubbing brushes. The Dockyard had its own railway system, complete with signals, platforms and locomotive sheds, to haul heavy iron plates, engines and guns from ships to workshops or to the building slipways.

In the Georgian era fine houses with stables and coach houses were built for senior Dockyard officials. There was a church, schools for apprentices, pay office and a guardhouse, a mortuary, beer bars, pigeon lofts, cookhouses, shops, surgeries and a fire station.

CENTURIES OF HISTORY

Over the centuries the Dockyard has remained in the forefront of technological developments - from the construction of the world's first dry dock in 1495 to the dawn of the industrial revolution, heralded by Brunel's steam-powered blockmaking factory in 1808.

The eyes of the world's navies were focussed on Portsmouth as the revolutionary Dreadnought battleships took shape in the early years of this century.

Throughout the First World War the Dockyard's massive workforce played a crucial role in winning the war at sea, building ships and submarines and quickly sending warships back to the battle after refits and repair work.

The Dockyard's record of service and dedication was repeated in full measure during the Second World War.

Portsmouth Dockyard in 1717

TOWN AND DOCKYARD

Close to the Dockyard was the Gunwharf where guns were serviced and stored, together with huge quantities of shot and shell. A fleet of lighters, manned by civilian crews, was responsible for the movement of ships, men and materials.

The Dockyard and the town of Portsmouth, which housed artisans, merchants and their families, were sufficiently important to justify strong defences and in the 1860s Lord Palmerston commissioned a string of forts to be built around the town and out in the Solent to defend Portsmouth. However, this threat was never realised and the forts became known as Palmerston's Follies.

Because the Dockyard was established beyond the town it was possible continuously to expand the area. When development started to surround to landward the great expansion of Victorian times could reclaim further land from the harbour.

In 1850 the 99 acre Portsmouth Dockyard was the world's biggest industrial centre, 17 acres having been added to build the steam basin, four docks and many large factories. But the coming of HMS *Warrior* and her ironclad sisters led to a massive expansion of the yard by a further 180 acres in 1864. The Historic Dockyard and Naval Base now occupy nearly 300 acres.

The visitor will quickly sense the atmosphere of permanence which prevails in Portsmouth Dockyard. It has outlasted kings and seen wars won and lost, spanning eight centuries of Britain's maritime and industrial history.

The Historic dockyard area with HMS Invincible *and HMS* Warrior *(1860) with HMS* Victory

1194–1550

In 1194 King Richard I ordered a dock to be built in Portsmouth and granted the town's first charter. Eighteen years later, on the instructions of King John, the Dockyard was enclosed "by a good and strong wall".

Portsmouth became the assembly point for attacks on France and the town was kept busy fitting out a series of royal expeditions. Portsmouth also suffered heavily in French retaliation raids.

The world's first dry dock was built here in 1495 and shipbuilding started on a large scale. One of the most famous ships to be built in Portsmouth was Henry VIII's flagship, *Mary Rose*, whose keel was laid down in 1509. Two years later Portsmouth was officially appointed as a building centre for the King's ships.

1550–1750

The great Tudor naval enterprises were followed by a century of stagnation. Then wars against the Dutch provided new work and the Dockyard was considerably enlarged. In 1670 Charles II created the Royal Navy and before the turn of the century a major expansion of Dockyard facilities was in progress. The Great Stone Dock, the Great Basin, building slips, wharfs and storehouses were built.

Artist's impression of King John's Dockyard in 1212

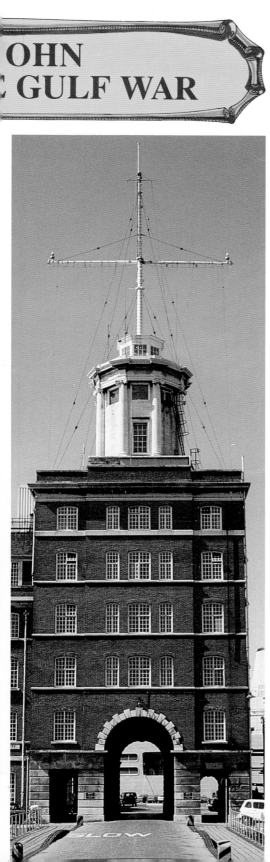

Semaphore Tower

1750–1850

The great age of sail and almost continuous warfare saw the Dockyard reach a new summit of importance although several serious fires hindered production. By 1800 the Royal Navy had 684 ships and the Dockyard was the world's largest industrial complex. Mechanisation was introduced when the first steam-powered factory for mass production of ships' blocks was established in 1802.

However, at the end of the Napoleonic wars hundreds of workers were laid off and by 1822 the workforce was reduced to 2,200. But this was only a temporary setback, for steam propulsion heralded the yard's greatest period of expansion and within 20 years the workforce had trebled. 1829 saw the launch of HMS *Fox,* the first steam screw warship built here.

1850–1900

The second half of the 19th century was marked by Dockyard expansion on a huge scale. Factories proliferated, new docks were built and in 1864 Parliament ordered 180 acres to be added to the Dockyard. HMS *Colossus,* the first steel ship to be built in Portsmouth, was launched in 1882. Ironically, during this period more than 2,000 men were discharged and given government help to emigrate to Canada.

1900 TO THE PRESENT

The dawn of the 20th century found the Dockyard embarked on building the revolutionary Dreadnought battleships. HMS *Dreadnought,* the first major ship to have steam turbines, was completed in the record time of a year and a day. More basins and locks were constructed and in 1913 the super-Dreadnought HMS *Queen Elizabeth,* the first oil-fired battleship, was launched. The story of the Dockyard's crucial support for the fleet in both World Wars is chronicled in later pages. In 1967 the frigate HMS *Andromeda* was the last warship built by Portsmouth Dockyard in a line of 286 known warships constructed here since 1497.

By 1978 the workforce had shrunk to 8,325. Further contraction was temporarily halted by the Falklands War in 1982. Nevertheless, two years later, with a civilian staff of 2,800, the Royal Dockyard was renamed the Naval Base Fleet Maintenance and Repair Organisation.

Victory Gate

Boathouses 5 & 6 and Mast Pond

Storehouses 9, 10 & 11

VICTORY GATE

Victory Gate, formerly Main Gate, was built with the Dockyard wall and completed in 1711. It was widened during the Second World War to allow large vehicles to enter and the wrought iron scrolled arch and lantern that spanned the two pillars was lost. Over the right-hand pedestrian entrance is a plaque surmounted by Queen Anne's Coat of Arms, which marks the Queen's visit in 1711. Just inside the gate to the right is the Porter's Lodge, built in 1708 and the Dockyard's oldest surviving building. Inside the left-hand pedestrian entrance is the Police Cell Block, built in 1882 for the detention of naval defaulters.

MAST POND AND BOATHOUSES

The Mast Pond was excavated in 1665 by soldiers, townsfolk and Dutch prisoners of war. Linked to the harbour by a tunnel under the road, it was originally used to store masts awaiting repair or collection. Now the Mast Pond is home to a collection of restored naval and other craft including an armed steam pinnace built in 1911. No 6 Boathouse, at the far end of the Pond, is a fine brick and stone building completed in 1846, and the two timber boathouses date from the late 19th century. The one on the right, No 5 Boathouse, contains the Mary Rose Exhibition.

STOREHOUSES

The three great naval storehouses along Main Road were built in the 1760s to house the ships' stores and equipment needed for Britain's rapidly expanding fleet. They were largely built by contractors re-using ships' timber, and all had brick cellars to protect inflammable materials. The elegant clocktower on the central storehouse was completed in 1992 and is a replica of the structure destroyed by German incendiary bombs during the 1941 blitz on Portsmouth. The weather vane, rescued from the rubble, has been restored and reset 100 ft above Portsmouth Harbour.

Naval Academy

THE NAVAL ACADEMY

The Naval Academy was the forerunner of Britannia Royal Naval College, Dartmouth. Completed in 1733, the college provided residential accommodation for a professor, governor and 40 students. At one time the fees equalled those of Eton and Westminster. George III ordered 15 places to be reserved for the sons of sea officers and to be paid for by the government. From 1906 to 1941 it was the Royal Naval School of Navigation. Bomb damage forced the school to move to Southwick House, north of Portsmouth, from where the invasion of Normandy was planned. The Academy is now an officers' mess.

THE PARADE

The Parade (Long Row) is a classic example of Dockyard housing constructed with elegance and style. Completed in 1719, it was designed by the Master Shipwright to house eight principal officers close to their place of work. To the rear of each house were servants quarters and substantial gardens. Most of the houses have now been converted into naval offices. The end house (No 9), now called Spithead House, was added in 1833 and became the residence of the Admiral Superintendent. Today it is the official home of Flag Officer Portsmouth.

The Parade (Long Row)

Dry Dock No 1 & HMS Invincible

THE GREAT SHIP BASIN

The Great Ship Basin and its six docks represent one of England's great legacies from the golden age of sail. Here was the hub of the Dockyard and the sight of the docks and basin filled with ships similar to HMS *Victory* would have been awesome. The basin and No 5 Dock date from 1698 and No 6 Dock came into use two years later. The basin was extended throughout the 1780s and the remaining dry docks were completed by 1802. When the basin was enlarged the original 1495 dock was uncovered. HMS *Victory* has occupied No 2 Dock since 1922 and the remains of the *Mary Rose* rest in No 3 Dock alongside.

MARY ROSE

The *Mary Rose* sank in the Solent on 19 July 1545, just over a mile from the dry dock where she was built for Henry VIII in 1509. She had served the King in his French campaigns for nearly 36 years before disaster struck. Heavily laden with troops, the ship took in water through her gun ports, heeled over and sank. Fewer than three dozen men survived.

During the excavation of the wreck more than 20,000 finds were recovered from the seabed and preserved by skilled scientists and conservators. The ship's massive hull presents a breathtaking spectacle in No 3 Dock beside HMS *Victory*.

Over 1,000 of the objects recovered from the ship are displayed in the *Mary Rose* Exhibition. They range from the Barber Surgeon's walnut medicine chest to archers' longbows. Bronze and wrought-iron guns are mounted on replicas of their original gun carriages, and visitors can also see a fascinating collection of the personal possessions of Tudor seamen.

City of Portsmouth

Mary Rose *Ship Hall*

HMS *VICTORY*

Already a veteran of three wars and four major battles when Nelson fought in her at the Battle of Trafalgar, HMS *Victory* is a monument to Britain's greatest naval battle and her brilliant Admiral, and offers her many visitors a unique insight into life in the Nelsonian navy. Having survived a demolition order, the ravages of teredo worm and death watch beetle, and even a German bomb in World War II, she is now being lovingly restored in one of the world's most ambitious ship preservation programmes.

The gracious setting of the Admiral's quarters contrasts with the rough messdecks where the ship's company lived, ate and slept. The maze of spars and rigging is a reminder of the remarkable seamanship of the era, while the gundecks, gloomy and packed with cannon, hint at the hardships that men endured both in and out of battle.

HMS *Victory* is still a fully commissioned ship and flies the flag of the Commander-in-Chief Naval Home Command.

City of Portsmouth

HMS Victory

HMS *WARRIOR*

HMS *Warrior* transformed battle fleets when she first appeared in 1860 as Britain's mighty answer to French ambitions to rule the waves. Her revolutionary concept was to house the main guns, boilers and engine in an impregnable armoured "box" or citadel. Her unique combination of iron hull, armourplate, breechloading guns and powerful engine meant that she could outgun and outrun any ship afloat and earned her the respect of Napoleon III who described her as "a black snake amongst rabbits".

However, she herself was obsolete within a few years although her hull survived in a number of roles, finally becoming a floating oil jetty at Pembroke Dock. HMS *Warrior* is now restored to her former glory and visitors can explore the huge gundeck where more than 400 sailors lived, worked and slept, as well as the captain's and officers' cabins, the wardroom, laundry, cells, engine and boiler rooms with a full-size working replica of the Penn engine.

City of Portsmouth

HMS Warrior

ROYAL NAVAL MUSEUM

Founded in 1911 as the Dockyard Museum and reorganised in 1938 as the Victory Museum, the Royal Naval Museum has now expanded to cover the whole spectrum of naval history - from the Middle Ages to the present. It concentrates above all on the people of the Royal Navy - ordinary seamen, Wrens and officers.

Housed predominantly on the ground floors of the Great Storehouses in the heart of the Historic Dockyard, the museum tells the story of the Senior Service in modern and vivid displays packed with fascinating naval treasures. A separate gallery houses HMS *Victory's* exhibition which covers the history of the ship and of her finest hour, the battle of Trafalgar.

Additionally, the museum possesses an extensive archive and library, which is available for use by researchers, and acts as an honourable repository for the medals, papers and other memorabilia of ex-naval personnel.

No visit to the great ships on display in the Historic Dockyard is complete without seeing the Royal Naval Museum.

R.N. Museum

The Royal Naval Museum

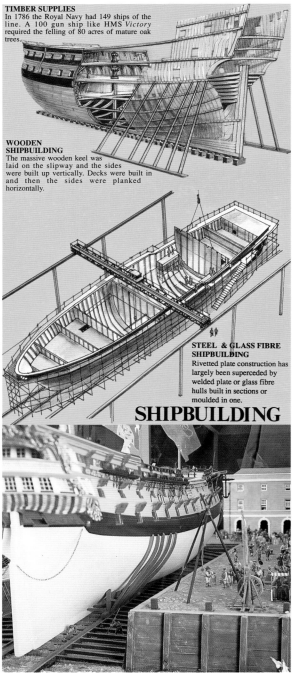

TIMBER SUPPLIES
In 1786 the Royal Navy had 149 ships of the line. A 100 gun ship like HMS *Victory* required the felling of 80 acres of mature oak trees.

WOODEN SHIPBUILDING
The massive wooden keel was laid on the slipway and the sides were built up vertically. Decks were built in and then the sides were planked horizontally.

STEEL & GLASS FIBRE SHIPBUILDING
Rivetted plate construction has largely been superceded by welded plate or glass fibre hulls built in sections or moulded in one.

SHIPBUILDING

The launch of HMS Warrior *at Portsmouth in 1781. Model by the late Clive Knight in the RN Museum*

EARLY DEVELOPMENTS

For centuries Portsmouth Dockyard remained in the forefront of maritime technological developments. As early as 1495 Henry VII ordered the construction of the world's first dry dock. By the 1690s the first stone wet and dry docks were being built and Portsmouth's Great Ship Basin and the six surrounding dry docks remain outstanding examples of docking facilities from the great age of sail.

THE INDUSTRIAL REVOLUTION

With the advent of steam and the Industrial Revolution, Portsmouth was again a leading creative force. A steam engine was installed in 1799 to pump water from the dry docks and three years later steam power was used to drive one of the first mechanical saw mills.

When the Great Basin was enlarged in 1802 the world's first caisson, or floating dam, was installed at its entrance. The caisson could be filled with water and sunk into the dock entrance to form a watertight seal. When it had to be moved it was pumped free of water and refloated. The caisson was wide enough to allow a roadway to be built on its top edge so that when sunk it formed part of the road, thus allowing workers and vehicles to move around the basin. By sealing the basin the docks could be used independently of the tides. During the 1860s, when the Dockyard was further enlarged, the first sliding caissons operated by compressed air were installed.

FIRST MASS PRODUCTION

However, these achievements were all overshadowed by the construction of Brunel's Block Mills, the world's first complete steam-powered factory. The blockmaking machinery, invented by Marc Brunel and manufactured by Henry Maudslay, was the first example of machine tools used for mass production. By 1808 forty-five machines were turning out 130,000 ships' pulley blocks a year. Ten unskilled men were able to equal the output of 100 blockmakers and the capital cost of the project was recovered in three years.

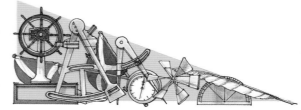

The Block Mills can be seen from the stern of HMS *Victory*. Some of Brunel's machines are still in the building, others are on display in the Science Museum and some are preserved by Portsmouth City Museum.

PIONEERS OF WARSHIP TECHNOLOGY

By 1805 Portsmouth was the principal yard for smelting and turning old copper into new ship fittings, and the pioneering work done in the metal mills enabled the yard to supply other dockyards with copper sheathing for ships' bottoms. A complex of foundries and patternmaking shops built in the 1850s enabled the yard to smelt any kind of metal and gave Portsmouth a unique edge to its refit and building capacities.

Portsmouth was again in the forefront by establishing a Technical Training School for Admiralty apprentices in 1809. In 1846 the first electrical lecturer was appointed, holding his office in the Chemical Laboratory. Portsmouth was the only Dockyard to have this facility, which greatly helped much of the pioneering work on naval ordnance developments. This work was carried out at the gunnery school of HMS *Excellent,* based on Whale Island in Portsmouth harbour and created from the spoil of excavations for new docks and basins in the Dockyard. The yard's technological expertise was also called upon for experimental and trials work when the Mine and Torpedo School was set up in HMS *Vernon*.

By the turn of the 20th century great engineering factories were being constructed and these performed much of the development work when the revolutionary HMS *Dreadnought* and her eight successors were built. Portsmouth was given the challenge of building many first-of-class warships and this earned the Dockyard an enviable "we can do it" reputation which still prevails today with the complex work on high-technology warships.

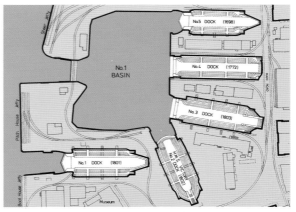
Plan of Basin No 1 and Dry Docks

Block Mills (1802)

Basin No 2

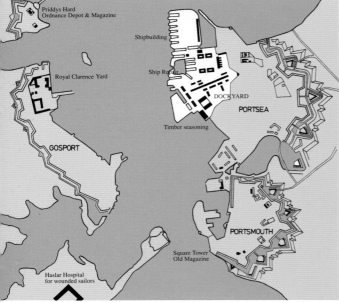

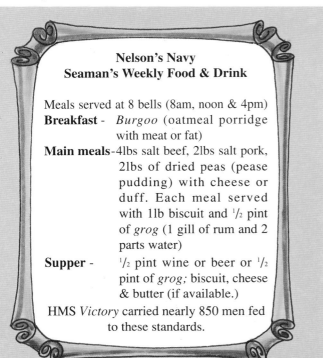

Stores establishments in Portsmouth and Gosport served the ships in harbour

---

Nelson's Navy
Seaman's Weekly Food & Drink

Meals served at 8 bells (8am, noon & 4pm)

Breakfast - *Burgoo* (oatmeal porridge with meat or fat)

Main meals - 4lbs salt beef, 2lbs salt pork, 2lbs of dried peas (pease pudding) with cheese or duff. Each meal served with 1lb biscuit and $\frac{1}{2}$ pint of *grog* (1 gill of rum and 2 parts water)

Supper - $\frac{1}{2}$ pint wine or beer or $\frac{1}{2}$ pint of *grog;* biscuit, cheese & butter (if available.)

HMS *Victory* carried nearly 850 men fed to these standards.

FEEDING THE NAVY

When fresh provisions were exhausted biscuits, salt beef, pork and fish, together with butter, cheese and beer formed the staple diet of British seamen fighting in the Napoleonic wars. This fare had changed little from Tudor times.

For centuries the supply of victuals came from private and government establishments in the town of Portsmouth. Breweries and bakeries were set up in the reign of Henry VIII to be followed by a cooperage, slaughterhouse, granaries and flourmills. The cooperage was transferred to Gosport in 1766.

MATERIAL SUPPLIES

To build, refit and store the great sailing fleet at the peak of the Napoleonic war the Dockyard needed materials to be transported by sea from all corners of the globe. It was not uncommon to see convoys of hundreds of ships laying at Spithead waiting to unload pine masting timbers from America or Scandinavia, iron from Sweden, mahogany from the Indies, tar and pitch from the Baltic.

Ships also brought copper and tin from the West Country for the foundries, iron cannon from the Tower armouries, oak from the forests of England, hemp for the ropehouses and canvas for the sail lofts.

The Great Storehouses bulged with materials including fittings made in the Dockyard. Equipment recovered from ships being laid up or in refit was renovated, stored and then reissued. Stores too large to be kept in buildings were laid apart in the anchor pound, boat pound and in timber grounds.

Demands of war and the growth of the fleet stretched the Victualling Board to breaking point and in 1827 an expansion programme started to centre all naval victualling in the Portsmouth area at Gosport. Four years later the new

establishment was named the Royal Clarence Yard. Today's food for the fleet, pre-packed, canned or deepfrozen, is kept in some of the original buildings across the harbour.

Clerks were employed to keep ledgers and handle the large sums of cash required every week to pay thousands of Dockyard workers. A new pay office, completed in 1808, was the Dockyard's first fireproof building, made from brick, stone and cast iron. Its interior remains largely unchanged. John Dickens, father of the novelist Charles Dickens, worked here as a pay clerk from 1809 to 1815. The Dickens family lived at 387 Mile End Terrace, Portsmouth, where Charles was born on 7 February 1812.

GUNS, POWDER AND SHOT

The Square Tower in Old Portsmouth, built in 1495, became the central powder magazine for the army and the fleet. However, storage and passage through the town of large amounts of gunpowder alarmed the residents and in 1767 they petitioned King George III for the removal of explosives to a more remote location.

The point was well made and shortly afterwards work started on the development of a basin, large magazine and ordnance buildings at Priddy's Hard, Gosport. Visitors to the Dockyard can look across the harbour and glimpse the old magazine which once contained 4,500 barrels of gunpowder.

By the 18th century the increase in size of Portsmouth's fortifications and the fleet led to the building of Gunwharf - later known as HMS *Vernon* - for the storage and servicing of shot and shell. In the late Victorian era Gunwarf became an elaborate arsenal and part of the Royal Ordnance. Large numbers of guns, including muskets and rifles, and piles of shot and shell were stored here.

Bridgeman Art Library

First Rate taking on stores by J.M.W. Turner

Anchors in Anchor lane

Armaments at Gunwharf

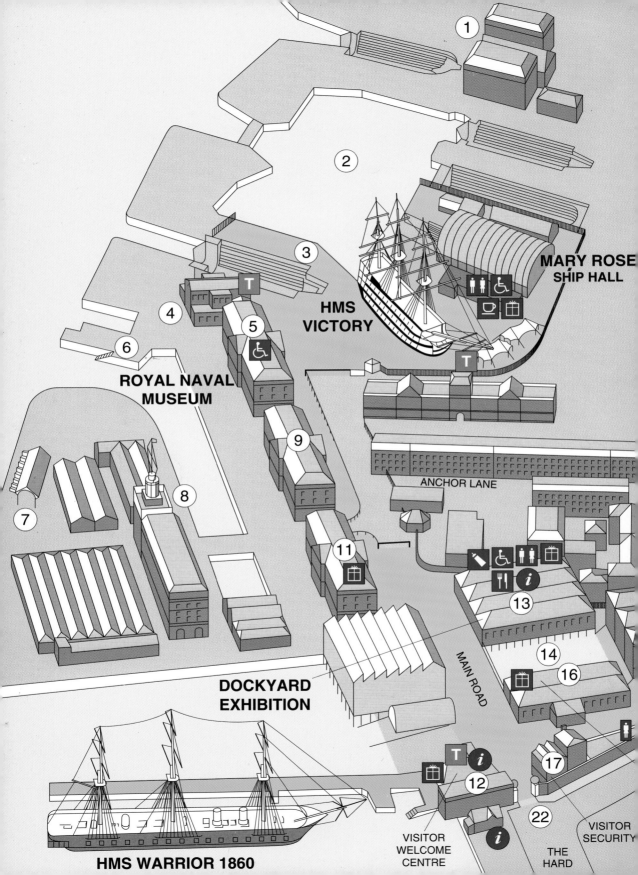

(1)

(2)

(3)

(4)

(5)

(6)

MARY ROSE SHIP HALL

HMS VICTORY

ROYAL NAVAL MUSEUM

(7)

(8)

(9)

(11)

ANCHOR LANE

(13)

(14)

(16)

DOCKYARD EXHIBITION

MAIN ROAD

(17)

(12)

(22)

HMS WARRIOR 1860

VISITOR WELCOME CENTRE

THE HARD

VISITOR SECURITY

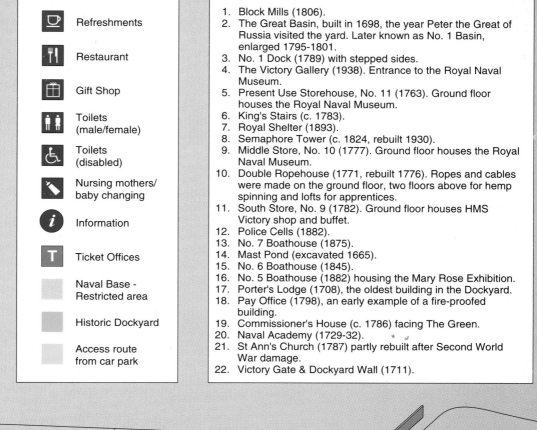

☕	Refreshments
🍴	Restaurant
🎁	Gift Shop
🚹	Toilets (male/female)
♿	Toilets (disabled)
🍼	Nursing mothers/ baby changing
i	Information
T	Ticket Offices
	Naval Base - Restricted area
	Historic Dockyard
	Access route from car park

1. Block Mills (1806).
2. The Great Basin, built in 1698, the year Peter the Great of Russia visited the yard. Later known as No. 1 Basin, enlarged 1795-1801.
3. No. 1 Dock (1789) with stepped sides.
4. The Victory Gallery (1938). Entrance to the Royal Naval Museum.
5. Present Use Storehouse, No. 11 (1763). Ground floor houses the Royal Naval Museum.
6. King's Stairs (c. 1783).
7. Royal Shelter (1893).
8. Semaphore Tower (c. 1824, rebuilt 1930).
9. Middle Store, No. 10 (1777). Ground floor houses the Royal Naval Museum.
10. Double Ropehouse (1771, rebuilt 1776). Ropes and cables were made on the ground floor, two floors above for hemp spinning and lofts for apprentices.
11. South Store, No. 9 (1782). Ground floor houses HMS Victory shop and buffet.
12. Police Cells (1882).
13. No. 7 Boathouse (1875).
14. Mast Pond (excavated 1665).
15. No. 6 Boathouse (1845).
16. No. 5 Boathouse (1882) housing the Mary Rose Exhibition.
17. Porter's Lodge (1708), the oldest building in the Dockyard.
18. Pay Office (1798), an early example of a fire-proofed building.
19. Commissioner's House (c. 1786) facing The Green.
20. Naval Academy (1729-32).
21. St Ann's Church (1787) partly rebuilt after Second World War damage.
22. Victory Gate & Dockyard Wall (1711).

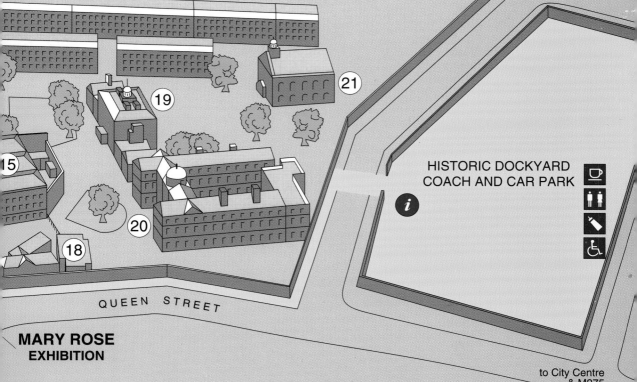

HISTORIC DOCKYARD
COACH AND CAR PARK

QUEEN STREET

MARY ROSE
EXHIBITION

to City Centre
& M275 →

Launch of a ship from Portsmouth in 1842

WOODEN SHIPS

It is generally acknowledged that many ships were built in Portsmouth before the first named ship, the *Sweepstake,* was launched in 1497. Since then nearly 300 vessels have been constructed here, without counting many rebuilds. This must be a record hard to equal.

The *Mary Rose,* built in 1509, was one of the largest ships of her time and the most famous of the early Portsmouth ships. She was remodelled in 1536 to become the first ship with broadside firing guns. This was the prototype of ship design for the next 350 years.

The 17th century was in many ways a formative period for the Royal Navy and the Dockyard. The administrative skills of Samuel Pepys transformed the Navy while master shipwrights such as Sir Anthony Deane, John Tippets and his son did much to lay the foundations of naval architecture. While serving at Portsmouth these men helped to establish the Dockyard's premier shipbuilding position that it was to retain until the 1940s.

When Admiral Anson circumnavigated the world in 1740-1744 his flagship was the Portsmouth-built *Centurion,* a 4th rate of 60 guns. During the Napoleonic war the yard fitted out many of the ships launched from private yards such as Bucklers Hard at Beaulieu, which had no docking or masting facilities.

STEAM AND STEEL SHIPS

Although a steam engine was introduced into the Dockyard in 1799, it was not until 1829 that Portsmouth built its first steam-powered warship, the 46-gun screw frigate *Fox.* In 1859 the *Royal Alfred* was the last timber hulled ship to be built at Portsmouth. She was armed with 10 nine-inch and 8 seven-inch rifled muzzle loading guns and an armoured belt which gave her a displacement of 6,700 tons.

Ships became larger and more powerful. HMS *Devastation,* Portsmouth's first iron ship laid down in 1869, displaced 9,380 tons and was considered to be the ultimate fighting ship. However, seven years later she was surpassed by the 11,800 ton *Inflexible,* armed by four 16-

Mary Rose *was launched at Portsmouth in 1509 and rebuilt here in 1536*

Launch of HMS London *(15,000 tons) in 1899*

inch guns and whose 24-inch thick armour has never been matched. The world rated her the most impregnable and lethal battleship.

The corvette *Calliope,* launched in 1884, won a miraculous battle against the elements. While she was in Samoa with six foreign warships and several merchantmen, a violent storm broke and one by one great waves carried the ships onto a reef. Captain Kane and his gallant crew inched the *Calliope* out of the harbour at a speed of one knot and she was the only ship to survive.

DREADNOUGHT BATTLESHIPS

Undoubtedly the most famous ship built in Portsmouth was the 17,900 ton battleship HMS *Dreadnought.* She was completed in a year and a day, a record never equalled for a ship of this size. *Dreadnought* was the first turbine driven warship and her revolutionary design rendered all other capital ships obsolete, starting a world-wide race to build bigger and more powerful battleships.

Between 1905 and 1915 Portsmouth built nine similar battleships - more than any other shipbuilding centre in the world. The *Queen Elizabeth* (27,500 tones) was the first oil-fired warship.

HMS Dreadnought *revolutionised battleship design in 1906*

SHIPS OF TWO WORLD WARS

After the First World War there were several lean years before Portsmouth embarked on a building programme dominated by cruisers such as *Suffolk, London* and *Dorsetshire.* HMS *Sirius,* a 5,600 ton anti-aircraft cruiser laid down in 1940 became Portsmouth's adopted warship. In 1964 the Dockyard built another *Sirius,* a Leander class frigate still serving with the fleet. Her sister ship, HMS *Andromeda* built in 1967, was the last in a long line of warships to be built in Portsmouth Dockyard.

HMS Sirius - *Portsmouth's adopted ship*

The Dockyard prepares for D-Day 1944

WORLD WAR I

Portsmouth Dockyard has actively responded to war for centuries but it was the two World Wars which brought the yard to its finest peak of service to the nation.

At the outbreak of the First World War, in August 1914, the Dockyard was already working flat out to complete great battleships for the Grand Fleet. The yard was stretched even further as the demands for war mounted. A manpower shortage crisis at the end of 1915 was caused by the increased workload and by many craftsmen volunteering for the fighting services.

For the first time women were recruited. Shortages became so acute that soon women from many walks of life donned overalls and became "Triangle Girls". Women on war service in the Dockyard all wore the distinctively shaped badge. By 1918 the yard was employing 23,000 people working day and night shifts.

During the four years of war the Dockyard refitted 1,200 vessels including 40 battleships, 25 cruisers, more than 400 destroyers, 150 torpedo boats, 140 trawlers and 20 submarines. It also built two battleships and five submarines. The Dockyard's strategic importance made it a prime target for enemy action and in September 1916 a Zeppelin bombed the yard.

HMS Invincible *returns from the Falklands War in August 1982*

The News

Dazzle camouflage was used in both World War I & World War II. Range finders, which rely on matching two half images, were difficult to use due to the geometric shapes on the ship's hull

WORLD WAR II

When the Second World War started in 1939 a reduced Dockyard workforce quickly set to work installing anti-aircraft guns on hundreds of trawlers and merchant ships. The battleship *Queen Elizabeth* was being rebuilt and many vessels were in for refit. Workers who had left the yard for the armed forces were recalled and the labour force spiralled to 25,000.

The fall of France, threat of invasion and bombing of the home counties in 1940 saw the Dockyard bursting with ships, many from occupied countries. Extra duties were thrust upon workers who doubled up as members of the Home Guard, the Auxiliary Fire Services or as air raid wardens and fire watchers.

Heavy bombing brought death and destruction to the City and Dockyard. It became dangerous to keep large ships in the yard so they were sent to safer yards in the north of England.

In 1944 Portsmouth became the assembly base for the invasion of Normandy, code-named "Operation Overlord". Armies and fleets gathered and engineers worked on the construction of the floating Mulberry Harbours and the famous Pluto pipeline which fed fuel under the sea to France. The Dockyard continued to work round the clock and by the end of the war 2,548 vessels had been dry-docked, repaired or refitted.

AFTER WORLD WAR II

In succeeding years lesser conflicts such as the Korean War, Suez, Borneo and Aden kept the Dockyard busy equipping the fleet for the nuclear age, but gradually defence cuts began to cast a dark shadow.

The Falklands War in 1982 showed the workforce at its best. Dockyard workers, some already issued with redundancy notices, laboured day and night to load thousands of tons of stores, fuel and ammunition, and to fit merchant ships with helicopter pads and guns. For the first time in history, television showed the world a taskforce on its way to war!

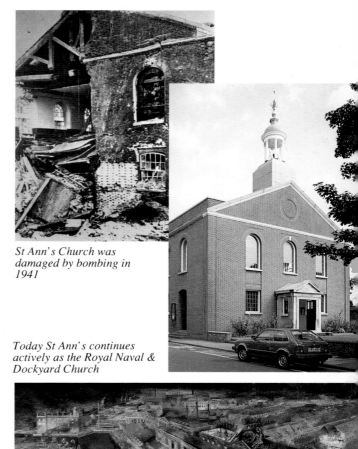

St Ann's Church was damaged by bombing in 1941

Today St Ann's continues actively as the Royal Naval & Dockyard Church

Tate Gallery

Richard Eurich's painting of a raid in 1941 which destroyed the clocktower on No 10 Storehouse

Similar view today

Short Row (1787) was built for Dockyard officers who needed to be on site

Admiralty House (1786) was built for the Commissioner of the Dockyard

Dockyard Sentry c1776 Regiment of Foot

Samuel Pepys of the Navy Board 1666

Dockyard Officer and son 1799

Dockyard Superintendent & wife 1830

LIVING IN THE DOCKYARD

For centuries Portsmouth Dockyard was literally a town within a town - a thriving community with factories, stores, offices, houses, schools and a church. The yard had its own police force, fire brigade and eventually a railway network. The workforce had also to care for livestock. There was stabling for horses, pigeon lofts - and generations of cats were fed by workers and sailors to keep down rats.

ELEGANT HOUSES

Close to their offices lived the officials who directed the large workforce, men like the Commissioner, the Master Shipwright and storekeepers. Fortunately, many of their elegant 18th century homes remain, some still occupied by naval staff.

Short Row is a pleasant terrace built in 1787 to house senior Dockyard officials. It was originally occupied by the Surgeon, Master Ropemaker, Clerk to the Ropeyard and the Boatswain.

Admiralty House is one of the Dockyard's outstanding buildings. Originally known as the Commissioner's House, it was completed in 1786 on a grand scale, to enable the Commissioner to accommodate and entertain distinguished visitors, including royalty. Although damaged by bombs in 1940-41, Admiralty House is little altered and today provides a residence and offices for the Commander-in-Chief Naval Home Command.

JACK THE PAINTER

The Great Ropehouse, fifth to be built in the Dockyard, was the victim of several disastrous fires which disrupted production of cordage for Britain's huge sailing navy in the 18th century. One of the outbreaks, in 1776, was caused by arson. The culprit, a Scot known as "Jack the Painter" hoped to help the cause of American Independence by crippling naval bases in England. He was tried at Winchester Assizes and hanged 60ft high from a mast set up just inside Victory Gate.

The Old Fire Station (1843) was housed beneath a large water tank supported by a cast iron structure. This old photograph was taken in 1898

FIRE BRIGADE

With so much inflammable material stored in the Dockyard a fire brigade was essential. The first mention of a fire engine was in 1664 when the Admiralty paid £20 for its provision. From 1843 the Fire Brigade was housed in a remarkable cast iron structure which is still known as the Old Fire Station. The building once supported a huge water tank used to feed fire-fighting mains.

CHURCH

St Ann's Church, built in 1787, has a light and graceful interior and is the only remaining Dockyard church still in use for regular worship. The west end was rebuilt in shortened form after bomb damage in the Second World War.

DOCKYARD RAILWAY

Horses moved heavy loads until steam locomotives replaced them c1860

The Dockyard had a railway as far back as the 16th century when horse drawn trolleys on wooden tracks were used to move heavy masts. A tramway system was laid down by the 1820s and with the growth of the Industrial Revolution the Dockyard developed a railway complex with steam locomotives replacing horses in the 1860s. For more than a century locomotives and wagons rolled round 25 miles of Dockyard track to serve the fleet. Trains also brought the royal family to the Dockyard to join the royal yacht, as well as bringing men to embark in troopships. The railway closed in 1977, but three railway wagons have been preserved as a reminder of the Dockyard's past and these will be displayed outside one of the storehouses on surviving track.

Generations of Dockyard cats fed by sailors and Dockyardmen kept down rats and mice.

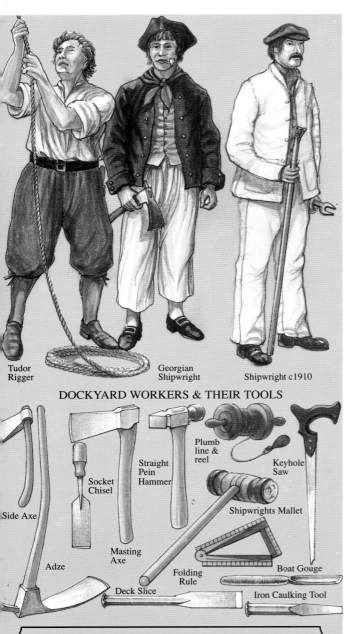

Tudor Rigger   Georgian Shipwright   Shipwright c1910

DOCKYARD WORKERS & THEIR TOOLS

Side Axe

Socket Chisel

Straight Pein Hammer

Plumb line & reel

Keyhole Saw

Shipwrights Mallet

Adze

Masting Axe

Folding Rule

Boat Gouge

Deck Slice

Iron Caulking Tool

SHIPWRIGHTS

The Dockyard's craftsmen have had to adapt to many changes, but none more so than the shipwright. He continues to dry dock ships and carries out all structural repairs in both wood and steel. Few ships are made of wood today, but the shipwright can still be seen on occasions using his traditional adze in the restoration of HMS *Victory*. Wood gave way to steel and now steel is being superseded by glass fibre, demanding an even wider range of skills from the shipwright.

ELECTRICIANS, FITTERS AND SAILMAKERS

Electricians are responsible for a wide range of tasks from simple lighting circuits to communications and complex weapon systems. Engine fitters have also seen many changes, for example the switch to gas turbines from steam engines. The fitter no longer works on the engine in the ship, but changes the gas turbine engine for an off-the-shelf replacement. The whole job takes just a few days.

Sailmakers and riggers still practise their old skills in splicing and needlework but, like the colour loft workers who make flags, they now use modern materials.

WELDERS AND BLACKSMITHS

The high quality steel used in warship construction demands great skill from the welders who join the plates together. Growth of the use of welding, however, has been at the expense of the blacksmith who manufactured many of the iron fittings needed on a ship.

Recording time was essential to assess a Dockyardman's pay. This time-clock is preserved in the Portsmouth Royal Dockyard Historical Society display

AT WORK

OTHER SKILLS AND CRAFTS
Nothing changes for joiners and french
polishers, who make ships' furniture, or for
plumbers and coppersmiths, but riveters have
almost disappeared from the Dockyard. They
have been replaced by iron caulkers who
prepare plating for the welders.

The job of storehousemen in issuing and
checking the thousands of items needed by a
modern warship can be just as demanding as
the work of those who maintain the dry docks,
vehicles and factories.

With the demise of the steam engine the
craft of the boilermaker has declined, but as
one skill wanes another takes its place,
ensuring the continued presence of the civilian
worker.

CHANGE OF NAME
On 1 October 1984 the Times obituary column
carried the following notice: "HM Royal
Dockyard Portsmouth passed peacefully away
at 12 o'clock last night after nearly 800 years of
faithful service. It will be sadly missed by
many". That day the Dockyard officially
became the Fleet Maintenance and Repair
Organisation with a reduced civilian workforce
of 2,800 working side by side with 500 Royal
Naval engineering personnel.

Although ships are no longer built here, the
yard remains a versatile repair base capable of
responding to a wide variety of tasks, and still
boasts its "we can do it" reputation.

VISITING NAVIES
Portsmouth's geographical position makes it a
popular port of call for visiting foreign
warships as well as for the Royal Navy. The
Dockyard, with its seven remaining dry docks,
four locks, stores and a highly-skilled
workforce, still gives its customers the same
spirit of co-operation and dedication which has
made it famous over the centuries.

City Planning, Portsmouth

A typical Dockyard scene

Builders of HMS Iron Duke *1912*

Dockyardmen leave work from Marlborough Gate c1898

HOME OF THE ROYAL NAVY

Portsmouth is the traditional home of the Royal Navy and visitors to the Historic Dockyard can glimpse today's sleek high-technology warships as they enter and leave the harbour, and sometimes at close quarters when berthed near HMS *Victory*. This blend of centuries-old vessels and contemporary fighting ships helps to make a visit to the Historic Dockyard a unique experience.

Although the working Dockyard has reduced its manpower, warships still depend on the support they get from dockyardmen and servicemen who work side by side to repair, maintain and supply them.

PORTSMOUTH SHIPS

Ships based at Portsmouth include the aircraft carriers HMS *Invincible, Illustrious* and *Ark Royal,* the assault ships *Fearless* and *Intrepid,* as well as Type-42 destroyers, frigates and a squadron of Hunt class mine countermeasures vessels.

The Royal Navy serves all over the world. From the South Atlantic to the Far East, from the Caribbean to the Gulf, the Royal Navy carries out its duties in fair weather and foul, in war and in peace. In the words of the naval prayer, it strives to be "a security for such as pass on the seas upon their lawful occasions".

Portsmouth hosts a large number of visits from NATO and other foreign warships and when crews stream ashore in unfamiliar uniforms they often mingle with visitors to the Historic Dockyard.

HMS Sirius

HMS Invincible

ROYAL NAVY

ROYAL FLEET AUXILIARY

Ships of the Royal Fleet Auxiliary are regular visitors to Portsmouth. Manned by the Merchant Navy and painted "battleship grey" the RFA tankers and supply ships are essential for the replenishment of the fleet at sea.

TUGS & TENDERS

Apart from the grey warships and auxiliaries, and the black hulls of conventional diesel-electric submarines based across the harbour at HMS *Dolphin,* various other types of craft can be seen.

Other ships with black hulls and buff superstructures belong to the Royal Maritime Auxiliary Service and carry out a wide variety of tasks. Tugs assist with berthing, fleet tenders carry stores and equipment and other specialist craft provide fuel and ammunition.

Other small craft painted black and grey are manned by volunteers of the Royal Naval Auxiliary Service.

THE ROYAL YACHT AND OTHER SHIPS

Two other Portsmouth-based ships have distinctive colours. The Royal Yacht *Britannia,* with three masts, a dark blue hull and white upperworks is well known world-wide, whilst the red hull of the Royal Navy's ice patrol ship makes her easy to spot amongst the Antarctic ice.

HMS Broadsword

HMS Fearless

Storehouse 10 clock tower was restored in 1992

PORTSMOUTH NAVAL BASE PROPERTY TRUST

The upkeep of the Historic Dockyard you have visited today is undertaken by the *Portsmouth Naval Base Property Trust,* a registered charity established in 1985. The Trust aims to preserve the historic buildings and docks so that everyone can enjoy them for many years to come. The Government has granted the Trust a long lease of the area, which includes many Ancient Monuments, and an initial sum of money to start the restoration works. However, much more money will be needed to complete restoration of the area and keep it maintained in good condition.

Rather than introduce an entrance charge to the Historic Dockyard, the Trust has chosen to raise the extra funds needed in other ways. For example, if you parked your car at the Historic Dockyard and Ships Car Park the fee you pay goes into the Trust's restoration fund. You have also contributed to the fund by purchasing this guidebook, which we hope you have found good value for money.

RESTORING BUILDINGS

Refurbishing the three Great Storehouses and reconstructing the clocktower on the roof of the central storehouse is, so far, the Property Trust's most important restoration project. The elegant clocktower was destroyed when enemy bombers attacked Portsmouth in 1941.

Extensive research into the design of the original 1776 structure has enabled a new clocktower to be built, resembling its predecessor as closely as possible. The weather vane is the only part of the former clocktower which survived the blitz. It was rescued from the rubble and now once more graces this important landmark.

John Lay & Co

High quality craftsmanship used to restore historic buildings

IMPROVING THE ATTRACTION

Portsmouth Dockyard, as it is today, provides many interesting things for the visitor to see and do, but the Trust is conscious that there are facilities that need to be improved to make your visit more comfortable. Over the next few years the Trust will be improving these facilities and introducing better catering and shopping.

The existing range of attractions will also be expanded to include new ticketing, orientation and education facilities, a new *Mary Rose* complex bringing the Ship Hall and the artifacts together, and a major attraction in No 6 Boathouse presenting many new displays, hands-on exhibits and a multi-media show.

PLANNING FOR THE FUTURE

A new building will house shops where you will be able to buy mementoes of your visit or a special gift, and new cafés and restaurants where you can sit and enjoy a meal overlooking Portsmouth Harbour. For those wanting a quick snack Boathouse No 7 will contain a food court with many different choices to tempt you.

Another important addition to the historic area over the next few years will be a brand new Museum of the Dockyard telling the story of the massive civilian workforce who built the ships, kept the Royal Navy afloat and played an important part in ensuring Britain's victory in two World Wars.

The Trust hopes you have enjoyed your visit. Do tell your family and friends about it, and if you have any comments or suggestions please write to us at the address below:

Portsmouth Naval Base Property Trust, 19 College Road, HM Naval Base, Portsmouth, PO1 3LJ.

Young visitors on the quarterdeck of HMS Victory

Proposals for Boathouse No. 6

FOLKLORE & SLANG

THE MYTHICAL BUGLER

Portsmouth Dockyard attracted considerable folklore and slang. Legend has it that when the mythical bugler sounds "return stores" the houses of Portsmouth will collapse and items stolen from the yard will march back to the Dockyard stores.

THE GOLDEN RIVET

The legend that every ship has a golden rivet meant that unsuspecting maidens were lured into the depths of a ship only to discover the "golden rivet" didn't exist and that their host's intentions were far from honourable. The following slang is a small part of Dockyard language.

Agony Stroke	Incident at a critical time.
All Bubbly?	"Is everything alright?"
Bell (the)	Muster bell.
Brow count	Record of men entering and leaving ships and recording time.
Chamfer up	Titivate a job to make it look better.
Clewing up	Finishing a job.
Coffin	Shipwright's tool box.
Cork Head	Person from the Isle of Wight.
Crab fat	Navy grey paint.
Drop of Thinners	"E needs a drop of thinners" i.e He is thick.
Gash	Waste material.
Greengrocer job	Job badly done.
Grot	Grotto. Unofficial hideaway hut.
Harry Taters	Job not done right.
Hungry One (or Seagull)	Man who will do anything to work overtime.
Key Press	M.O.D. Police keyboard.
Lammy	Short, single breasted coat with 2 pockets. Made of Fearnought material in the Dockyard.
Legacy	Nasty job left by someone else.
Matey	Dockyardman. Abbr: for His/Her Majesty's Dockyardman.
Muster	In or out muster. To clock in or out of the Dockyard.
Oggin	Sea water or sea. "E fell in the 'oggin." (Navy Term).
Party	Gang of workmen.
Poultice Walloper	First Aid Man.
Saga	Small job that becomes a large one.
Silent Hours	Lunchtime. When work stops.
Ticklers	Hand rolled cigarettes.
Tiddly	Something that looks smart or nice.
Turk Head	Person from Gosport.
West Oh	Person from Plymouth.
Yard	The Dockyard.

(Extracted from "A Dictionary of Dockyard Language" by B.H. Patterson of the Portsmouth Royal Dockyard Historical Society.)

ACKNOWLEDGEMENTS

The Portsmouth Naval Base Property Trust wishes to thank Coopers and Lybrand, Chartered Accountants and Management Consultants, one of the leading providers of financial and business advisory services in the UK for their sponsorship of this publication.

© Portsmouth Naval Base Property Trust 1992

Design: Graham Bishop, City Planning, Portsmouth
ISBN 0 85372 618 3   395/10

History: Brian Patterson, Portsmouth Royal Dockyard Historical Society; Jonathan Coad, English Heritage.

This publication is dedicated to the memory of its designer, Graham Bishop, a friend and major contributor to the work of the Property Trust.

Published for the Portsmouth Naval Base Property Trust by Pitkin Pictorials, Andover, Hampshire.

Printed in Great Britain.